Amish Home

RAYMOND BIAL

Houghton Mifflin Company
Boston

Acknowledgments

I would like to thank Mary Lee Donovan, Walter Lorraine, Laura Hornik, Amy Bernstein, Audrey Bryant, and the other staff at Houghton Mifflin for their support and assistance with this project.

I would also like to thank Rebecca Mabry for permission to reprint quotes from her fine series of articles, "Be Ye Separate: A Look at the Illinois Amish," published in the *News-Gazette* (Champaign, Illinois).

I am deeply indebted as well to the Amish families who allowed me to photograph in and around their homes, even though I was a stranger arriving with an assortment of cameras. I promised not to photograph the families themselves, and in return was offered what mattered most to me — their implicit trust. It was rarely spoken of, except for an occasional smile, shy glance, and quiet gesture of welcome, yet our brief acquaintance led to a sense of mutual respect that I will always carry with me.

Library of Congress Cataloging-in-Publication Data

Bial, Raymond.
  Amish home / Raymond Bial.
    p.   cm.
    Summary: Text and photographs depict the way of life of the Amish.
    HC ISBN 0-395-59504-5   PA ISBN 0-395-72021-4
  1. Amish — Social life and customs — Pictorial works. 2. Amish — Social life and customs.   [1. Amish.]   I. Title.
E184.M45B52 1993   92-4406
973'.08'8287 — dc20   CIP
                    AC

Printed in the United States of America
HOR 10 9 8 7 6 5 4 3

This book is lovingly dedicated to my wife,
Linda, the significance of whose presence in my life
can be neither overstated nor overvalued.

Author's note

The Amish do not allow themselves to be photographed because of the biblical passage cautioning against the making of "graven images" and because of *Gelassenheit,* a German word that roughly means "humility." They believe that it is prideful to draw attention to themselves. As one Amish lady told me, "You may not take any pictures of me, but you may photograph anything I own, because worldly goods do not matter to me." Another young man, as he shoed a workhorse, shyly grinned and remarked, "Sure, you can take all the photographs you want, just so I don't get in any of them!"

Out of respect for these gentle and industrious people, there are no portraits in this book. Yet one can also know people by their crafts, and there are many photographs of buggies, quilts, clothing, and other possessions in *Amish Home.* Although the Amish do not place any value on these "worldly goods," they are hardworking, productive people, and the objects around them very much reflect the spirit of their lives.

When visiting an Amish settlement, you may at first think that you are traveling down any country road. The sun gleams on the ribbon of asphalt. Queen Anne's lace and black-eyed Susans crowd the shoulder, and the fields unfold green in every direction. However, as you drive along, you quickly discover that you have entered another world.

You may first notice a horse and buggy clip-clopping along the road. Among the Amish, the horse and buggy serve not only as a practical means of transportation, but as symbols of their way of life, because these deeply religious people do not believe in owning and driving automobiles.

Many people consider the Amish to be old-fashioned because they have rejected much of modern technology, including radios and televisions. Actually, the Amish do not oppose progress so much as they conscientiously adhere to their own beliefs. These beliefs are rooted in their religion, which emphasizes the importance of family and community, and their agrarian way of life. Far from being "the plain people," as they are often called, the Amish live in accordance with a complex and dynamic system of values.

For the sake of their community the Amish have given up many individual freedoms, and they do not value material wealth. But unlike the Puritans and other ascetic religious groups, they do not believe in depriving themselves. They enjoy good food and many social activities. They are genuinely pleasant and respectful to friend and stranger alike. They love their children and have added many touches of humor, originality, and beauty to their lives.

Believing that they must live apart, the Amish consider themselves to be "in the world, but not of it." Whether parked in the yard, sheltered in a barn, or moving slowly down a country road, their buggies demonstrate that they have prevailed over worldly progress and that they are unlike others, to whom they refer collectively as the "English." Among themselves, the Amish speak a dialect similar to Low German and conduct religious services in a language similar to High German. With others, they speak English.

Because they cannot easily travel more than a few miles in their buggies, the Amish remain near home and visit relatives and friends within their closely knit rural community. The Amish cherish their families and their neighbors, and visiting is an integral part of their lives.

Amish settlements are divided into church districts. Each congregation, or *Gemeinde,* within a district has between fifteen and thirty families, or about seventy-five baptized adult members. Generally, there is one bishop in each congregation, along with two or three preachers and a deacon.

The families in each congregation live near one another, basically no farther than a horse and buggy can comfortably travel to worship services. Every other Sunday, members gather in each other's homes because the Amish do not have formal church buildings. (Alternate Sundays are reserved for visiting friends and relatives.) Hymnbooks, benches, dishes, silverware, and everything else needed for services and the dinner afterward are carried to the homes in church wagons.

Amish buggies are made in a simple, box-like design that represents the lack of pretension in the lives of the Amish. Bases and frames of the buggies are now constructed of fiberglass, which is more durable than wood. Buggies may sport other modern features such as vinyl tops, ball-bearing wheels, hydraulic brakes, and battery-powered windshield wipers. They are also outfitted with fluorescent triangles and reflector lights for safety. Some Amish install carpet and upholstery in one of several colors, which might be considered "fancy." However, these innovations are permitted as long as the basic design of the buggies remains unchanged.

Buggy styles and colors vary from one region to another, yet these are simply variations on the theme of "plain living." Costing as much as $3,000, the buggies are made in special shops. It may take a full ten days to build one, but the buggy can last for a lifetime.

During their teenage years, many Amish boys go through a wild period called *rumpaspringa,* which means "jumping around" or "running around." They may soup up their buggies with plastic reflectors, stereos, carpeting, dashboards, and speedometers. Parents and church leaders tolerate this flouting of rules so their children can get a taste of the outside world and then decide for themselves whether or not they wish to be baptized as adults into the Amish faith. With a good horse, buggies usually travel 12 mph. With an older horse they may average 10 mph, but if you ever clock one going 15 mph, one Amishman quipped, "you can be sure it's a teenage driver!"

Horses also symbolize Amish culture and values. The animals are seemingly everywhere—grazing in pastures of sweet grass, congregating in barnyards, and taking advantage of shade trees along fencerows. If they are sleek animals, they are likely Standardbreds used to pull buggies. These horses are often retired harness racers, and the Amish appreciate their grace and spirit. Most Amish keep one or two driving horses.

Large, muscular draft horses with clumpy hooves are used for fieldwork. Amish farmers often have six to eight of these horses, because they may use tractors only in their farmyards as power sources for jobs such as grinding feed and transporting ear corn into cribs.

The Amish do not use tractors for fieldwork because of high equipment and fuel costs. They are quick to point out that horses replace themselves, while other farmers must purchase an expensive new tractor every few years. In addition, the manure

of horses and other livestock is useful as fertilizer, though chemical fertilizers are sometimes used as well. The Amish know that high production costs would require them to expand the size of their farms, and the only way to do so would be at the expense of their neighbors. Smaller farms enable the Amish to live closer to one another in their rural communities.

During the spring, Amishmen competently guide the powerful horses over the bare fields as they plow, harrow, and plant their crops. Horses are also used to cultivate and harvest crops, as well as to bale hay and straw. The Amish care deeply about their land and follow sound farming practices such as crop rotation. They are particularly adept at transforming land of poor fertility into productive farms. Acre for acre, they are among the best farmers on earth.

In Amish country you may next notice what is *not* there. No utility lines are strung to the houses, because the Amish cannot have electricity in their homes. The Amish do not object to electricity itself, which may be used in woodworking and related businesses. They simply do not want television and radio to threaten family life. As one Amishman noted about his English neighbors, "The center of attention in their home is the tube. They're home together, but they're not sharing anything."

The Amish spend their leisure time reading books and magazines. They do not believe in formal education beyond eighth grade, because they prefer to concentrate on practical skills that will be of greatest value to them as farmers, housewives, and craftsmen. Yet the Amish are hardly opposed to learning and they are generally better informed about world events than many of their English neighbors.

The Amish also do not permit telephones in their homes, although they may use their English neighbors' phones, pay telephones, or special phones placed in small wooden buildings along country roads. They are not opposed to the telephone itself, but to its convenience. If they had the devices in their homes, they fear that people would not go to the trouble of hitching a horse to a buggy and driving down the road to visit a friend or relative.

On the outside, Amish homes appear similar to others in the region. They are generally painted white, with no shutters or fancy trim. What distinguishes them most visibly are the blue or green curtains. The bright colors might be considered fancy, but as long as the fabric is not patterned, they are acceptable.

The Amish have always preferred to be farmers, because of the biblical directive that man should live "by the sweat of his brow." They also believe that living on the land brings them closer to God. In recent years, however, with growing families and the high cost of farmland, they have been forced to work in various trades in order to support their families. The changes have been permitted, as long as the men continue to work with their hands. The Amish have proven to be skilled craftsmen, and their products are highly valued.

The Amish originally came from Europe, where they were persecuted for many years. Like Martin Luther and others in the Reformation, they broke away from the Catholic Church, believing that religion was a matter of individual conscience and that they should emulate the peaceful example of Jesus Christ regardless of the cost. To this day, alongside the Bible, virtually every Amish family reserves a special place in its home for a book called *Martyr's Mirror,* which chronicles the suffering of their ancestors during those early years in Europe.

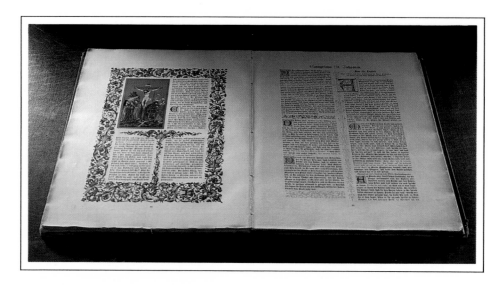

Seeking religious freedom, the first Amish settled in Pennsylvania in the early 1700's. Although they do not actively seek new members, their population has grown because they have large families, averaging seven or eight children. There are now more than 100,000 Amish living in twenty-five states, primarily in Pennsylvania, Ohio, Indiana, Illinois, and Iowa. No Amish remain in Europe, although they originated there.

The Amish did not appear overly different from their English neighbors until the early twentieth century. As the rest of the country bought Model T automobiles, they continued to drive their horses and buggies. Believing that "the old is the best," the Amish also did not change their dress, at least not outwardly, while the rest of the world embraced the latest styles.

Along with the horse and buggy, their clothing reflects how the Amish actually live their faith. Considering themselves to be plain people, the Amish are not allowed to wear patterns, which are considered fancy, even prideful. However, unlike the Puritans of early America, the Amish are not prevented from literally bringing a little color into their lives. On washdays, purple, royal blue, green, orange, and other brightly colored dresses hang on clotheslines in every yard. Turquoise and lime green shirts worn by men and boys also flap in the breeze.

Amish women make all of the clothing for their families, using treadle sewing machines and brown paper patterns handed down through the generations. Today, however, polyester fabrics have largely replaced cotton and wool. These permanent press materials have brought some convenience to Amish housewives, many of whom still use heavy flatirons (also called sad irons), which are heated on the burners of wood or gas stoves.

Their dress identifies the Amish as members of a particular group, just as some professionals, such as nurses, wear uniforms. Through standardized dress and hair style the Amish express loyalty to their community. Plain clothing ensures humility as well: by surrendering control over their appearance, the Amish demonstrate that they as individuals are less important than the group.

When the Amish broke away from the Mennonites in the late 1600's, the Amish rejected buttons as too fancy. The Mennonites came to be known as the "button people" and the Amish as the "hook and eyers." This tradition is so strong that to this day Amish girls and women still fasten their dresses with straight pins. Amish boys and men still rely on hooks and eyes on their coats and jackets.

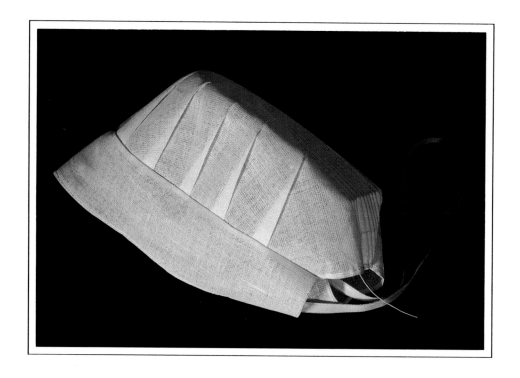

From the age of eight, Amish girls wear aprons and triangular capes over their dresses, both of which indicate modesty. The apron is large enough to cover pregnant women, and the cape allows mothers to nurse their babies discreetly. Amish women also wear a white prayer *kapp,* or cap, made of Swiss organdy, often with a bonnet. The head coverings symbolize deference to God and to man. Men do occupy leadership positions in Amish society, including head of household, and both men and women have clearly defined roles. Men and women are considered equal partners, however, and they treat each other with the deepest respect. Amish women co-own farms with their husbands and manage all financial matters in their families.

Amish boys wear dresses until they are about one year old, when they switch to pants and shirts. At age four, boys begin to wear adult-style suits, which include a vest, suspenders, coat, hat, and broadfall trousers, sometimes called "barn-door britches." For the sake of modesty, the trousers are held up by suspenders so they won't have to fit tightly at the waist. Instead of a zipper in the front, the pants have a wide flap that is closed with hooks or buttons at the sides.

Among men, the wide-brimmed hat is perhaps the most recognizable symbol of Amish dress. Starting at the age of two, boys wear straw hats in the summer and black felt hats or stocking caps in the winter. Outside the home, hats are worn nearly all the time.

Amish women never cut their hair, which is braided and knotted at the back, while the hair of Amish boys and men is cut to the ear and not parted. Amish men must be clean-shaven until they are married, at which time they must grow full beards, without mustaches. They do not wear mustaches because centuries ago in Europe soldiers wore them, and pacifism is fundamental to Amish beliefs.

Because they raise most of their own food, the Amish enjoy the abundance and independence of rural life. Their large, carefully tended vegetable gardens do not have a single weed.

The Amish butcher their own cattle, pigs, and chickens, and every year can and freeze huge amounts of meat. They also put up bushels of produce, filling up their cellars for the winter and often renting locker space in town. Families purchase only staples, such as flour, sugar, and coffee, at the grocery store. They may spend as little as $25 every two weeks for a family with seven or more children.

Like those of the English, Amish homes have kitchens, bedrooms, living rooms, and modern bathrooms. Downstairs rooms are large, however, with wide doorways or movable walls that can be opened up to accommodate large groups for religious services. All of the furniture is plain, with no print patterns. Only calendars and framed religious sayings are permitted on the walls; years ago, church rules forbade mirrors as well as pictures.

Kitchens are typically filled with cabinets made by local Amish craftsmen. Until recently, all kitchens contained wood stoves, dry sinks, and hand pumps; there were no refrigerators or modern stoves. Today, however, many Amish homes have these appliances, as well as washing machines and dryers, powered by natural gas. They are allowed to use gas but not electricity because, as the Amish wryly point out, no one has yet figured out a way to run a television set on natural gas. In fact, because they often cook for large groups of people, many Amish housewives now have *two* stoves and refrigerators.

Coleman and propane lanterns are now used to light Amish homes, having replaced more traditional oil lamps, although they may still adorn mantels as decorations. Lanterns take a few moments to light, but they illuminate as well as a 100-watt bulb.

Traditionally, the Amish have relied on wood heat, but many homes are now equipped with gas stoves located in the living room. The Amish do not have central heating, viewing it as an unnecessary comfort. Bedrooms are plainly furnished, except for a handsome quilt on the bed. During the winter, these upstairs rooms become quite cold.

Many Amish women spend their "spare time" making quilts, and it is common to see a quilt in progress spread out in the living room. These lovely quilts do not depict flowers, animals, people, or other representational designs, yet the women manage to compose strikingly original geometric patterns with bright, strong colors. Highly prized by other Amish and the English alike, their quilts are used at home or offered for sale to supplement the income of their large families.

Just as they enjoy informal visiting, the Amish look forward
to gatherings of large groups for worship or major work projects
such as quilting bees or barn raisings. Much of the work is labor
intensive and could be done more easily with modern machines.
However, the Amish reason that it is better for a group to work
together than for an individual to labor alone. They also love
group games such as baseball and volleyball. Whether for work
or fun, these events are all commonly referred to as "frolics."

This life may appear to be idyllic, but the Amish do have
occasional problems with crime and divorce. As one Amishman
said, "It's not all pie and cakes." About 20 percent of young
people choose to join a less demanding denomination or to
leave the Amish faith altogether, and "go English."

Although they have attempted to remain separate from the world, the Amish have at times found themselves in serious conflict with the society around them. Because of their belief in pacifism, for example, they have been mistreated, even imprisoned, for their refusal to participate in wars.

They also came into deep conflict with school officials because they do not formally educate their children beyond eighth grade. Once Amish children attended one-room schools along with their English neighbors, but as schools began to consolidate, the Amish saw them as a threat to their way of life. They successfully established their own schools and have proved to be very competent educators.

Because they believe in taking care of themselves, the Amish have been exempted from social security tax. For years they paid into the fund but refused to accept benefits. They do not have insurance and rarely send old people to nursing homes. When

they get too old to work, Amish men and women move into adjoining houses called *grossdadi* houses, where they are cared for by their children.

As much as they wish to separate themselves from the world, the Amish do take advantage of hospitals and use public roads. They have clearly accepted many technological innovations, while rejecting others. They believe that they have maintained control over their lives, while other people have allowed their lives to be shaped by technology.

Historically, many people have made fun of the Amish simply because they lived differently. In recent years, however, many people have come to respect Amish ways. As a consequence, their settlements have become prime tourist attractions. The Amish have been dismayed by the intrusions, yet they also realize that their own livelihood depends in part on tourists who stop by to purchase handmade goods and fresh produce.

Certainly, despite their outward appearance, the Amish have not remained unchanged over the years. They aren't as "plain" as they appear to be, and they are not without their difficulties. In their world the individual occupies a small place, but is always valued. In the larger culture, the individual is foremost, yet people often feel isolated and alone.

In many ways, the Amish have remained "in this world, but not of it." Perhaps the clearest insight will come from understanding both their world *and* ours. Just as the Amish have learned many lessons from those around them, they also have much to teach us, simply by their example.

Further Reading

The following books, periodicals, and newspaper articles were consulted in the preparation of *Amish Home:*

Good, Merle, and Good, Phyllis. *Twenty Most Asked Questions about the Amish and Mennonites.* Lancaster, Pa.: Good Books, 1979.

Hostetler, John A. *Amish Life,* 2d ed. Scottsdale, Pa.: Herald Press, 1983.

Hostetler, John A. *Amish Society,* 3d ed. Baltimore: Johns Hopkins University Press, 1980.

Hostetler, John A., ed. *Amish Roots: A Treasury of History, Wisdom, and Lore.* Baltimore: Johns Hopkins University Press, 1989.

Kline, David. *Great Possessions: An Amish Farmer's Journal.* San Francisco: North Point Press, 1990.

Kraybill, Donald B. *The Riddle of Amish Culture.* Baltimore: Johns Hopkins University Press, 1989.

Meyer, Carolyn. *Amish People: Plain Living in a Complex World.* New York: Atheneum, 1977.

Scott, Stephen. *The Amish Wedding and Other Special Occasions of the Old Order Communities.* Intercourse, Pa.: Good Books, 1988.

Scott, Stephen, and Pelman, Kenneth. *Living without Electricity.* Intercourse, Pa.: Good Books, 1990.

Warner, James A., and Denlinger, Donald M. *The Gentle People: A Portrait of the Amish.* Lancaster, Pa.: Stel-Mar, 1982.

Cobblestone: The History Magazine for Young People v. 8, no. 11, November, 1987 (Special issue devoted to the Amish).

Mabry, Rebecca. "Be Ye Separate: A Look at the Illinois Amish." Champaign, Ill.: *News-Gazette,* 1989 (Reprint of a series of newspaper articles).

Young readers may also enjoy the following books about the Amish:

Ammon, Richard. *Growing Up Amish.* New York: Macmillan, 1990.

Israel, Fred L. *The Amish.* New York: Chelsea House Publishers, 1986.

Naylor, Phyllis Reynolds. *An Amish Family.* New York: Amereon House, 1986.